CHRISTIAN BEHAVIOUR

By C. S. Lewis

The Screwtape Letters

The Case for Christianity

The Problem of Pain

Christian Behaviour

CHRISTIAN BEHAVIOUR

BY

C. S. LEWIS

Fellow of Magdalen College, Oxford

A Further Series of Broadcast Talks

NEW YORK

THE MACMILLAN COMPANY

1948

Copyright, 1943, by
THE MACMILLAN COMPANY

———

———

Eighth Printing

PRINTED IN THE UNITED STATES OF AMERICA
BY THE VAIL-BALLOU PRESS, INC., BINGHAMTON, N. Y.

CONTENTS

I

THE THREE PARTS OF MORALITY

THERE'S a story about a schoolboy who was asked what he thought God was like. He replied that, as far as he could make out, God was "The sort of person who is always snooping round to see if anyone is enjoying himself and then trying to stop it." And I am afraid that is the sort of idea that the word Morality raises in a good many people's minds: something that interferes, something that stops you having a good time. In reality, moral rules are directions for running the human machine. Every moral rule is there to prevent a breakdown, or a strain, or a friction, in the running of that machine. That is why these rules at first seem to be constantly interfering with our natural inclinations. When you're being taught how to use any machine, the instructor keeps on saying, "No, don't do it like that," because, of course, there are all sorts of things that look all right and seem to you the natural way of treating the machine, but don't really work.

Now let us go a step further. There are two ways in which the human machine goes wrong. One is when human individuals drift apart from one another, or else collide with one another and do one another damage, by cheating or bullying. The other is when things go wrong inside the individual—when the different parts of him (his different faculties and desires and so on) either drift apart or interfere with one another. You can get the idea plain if you think of us as a fleet of ships sailing in formation. The voyage will be a success only, in the first place, if the ships don't collide and get in one another's way; and, secondly, if each ship is seaworthy and has her engines in good order. As a matter of fact, you can't have either of these two things without the other. If the ships keep on having collisions they won't remain seaworthy very long. On the other hand, if their steering gears are out of order they won't be able to avoid collisions. Or, if you like, think of humanity as a band playing a tune. To get a good result, you need two things. Each player's individual instrument must be in tune, and also each must come in at the right moment so as to combine with all the others.

But there is one thing we haven't yet taken into account. We haven't asked where the fleet is trying to get to, or what piece of music the band is trying to play. The instruments might be all in tune and might all come in at the right moment, but even so the performance wouldn't be a success if they had been engaged to provide dance music and actually played nothing but Dead Marches. And however well the fleet sailed, its voyage would be a failure if it were meant to reach New York and actually arrived at Calcutta.

Morality, then, seems to be concerned with three things. Firstly, with fair play and harmony between individuals. Secondly, with what might be called tidying up or harmonising the things inside each individual. Thirdly, with the general purpose of human life as a whole: what man was made for: what course the whole fleet ought to be on: what tune the conductor of the band wants it to play.

2

You may have noticed that modern people are nearly always thinking about the first thing and forgetting the other two. When people say in the newspapers that we are fighting for Christian moral standards, they usually mean that we are fighting for kindness and fair play between nations, and classes, and individuals; that is, they're thinking only of the first thing. When a man says about something he wants to do, "It can't be wrong because it doesn't do anyone else any harm," he's thinking only of the first thing. He's thinking it doesn't matter what his ship is like inside provided that he doesn't run into the next ship. And it is quite natural, when we start thinking about morality, to begin with the first thing, with social relations. For one thing, the results of bad morality in that sphere are so obvious and press on us every day: war and poverty and graft and quislings and shoddy work. And also, as long as you stick to the first thing, there is very little disagreement about morality. Almost all people at all times have agreed (in theory) that human beings ought to be honest and kind and helpful to one another. But though it is natural to begin with all that, if our thinking about morality stops there, we might just as well not have thought at all. Unless we go on to the second thing—the tidying up inside each human being—we are only deceiving ourselves.

What is the good of telling the ships how to steer so as to avoid collisions if, in fact, they're such crazy old tubs that they can't be steered at all? What's the good of drawing up, on paper, rules for social behaviour, if we know that, in fact, our greed, cowardice, ill temper, and self-conceit are going to prevent us from keeping them? I don't mean for a moment that we oughtn't to think, and think hard, about improvements in our social and economic system. What I do mean is that all that thinking will be mere moonshine unless we realise that nothing but the courage and unselfishness of individuals is ever going to make any system work properly. It is easy enough to remove the particular kinds of graft or bullying that go on under the present system: but as long as men are twisters or bullies they will find some new way of carrying on the old game under the new system. You can't make men good by law: and without good men you can't have a good society. That is why we must go on to think of the second thing: of morality *inside* the individual.

But I do not think we can stop there either. We are now getting to the point at which different beliefs about the universe lead to different moralities. And it would seem, at first sight, very sensible to stop before we got there, and just carry on with those parts of morality that all sensible people agree about. But can we? Remember that religion involves a series of statements about fact, which must be either true or false. If they are true, one set of conclusions will follow about the right sailing of the human fleet: if they are false, quite a different set. For example, let us go back to the man who says that a thing can't be wrong unless it hurts some other human being. He quite understands that he mustn't damage the other ships in the convoy, but he honestly thinks that what he does to his own ship is simply his own business. But does it not make a great difference whether it really *is* his own ship or not? Doesn't it make a great difference whether I am, so to speak, the landlord of my own mind and body, or only a tenant, responsible to the real landlord? If somebody else made me, for his own purposes, then I shall have a lot of duties which I should not have if I simply belonged to myself.

Again, Christianity asserts that every individual human being is going to live for ever, and this must be either true or false. Now there are a good many things which wouldn't be worth bothering about if I were going to live only seventy years, but which I'd better bother about very seriously if I am going to live for ever. Perhaps my bad temper or my jealousy are gradually getting worse—so gradually that the increase in seventy years won't be very noticeable. But it might be absolute *hell* in a million years: in fact, if Christianity is true, hell is the precisely correct technical term for what it would be. And immortality makes this other difference, which, by the by, has a connection with the difference between totalitarianism and democracy. If individuals live only seventy years, then a state, or a nation, or a civilisation, which may last for a thousand years, is more important than an individual. But if Christianity is true, then the individual is not only more important but incomparably more important, for he is everlasting and the life of a state or a civilisation, compared with his, is only a moment.

It seems, then, that if we are to think about morality, we must think of all three departments: relations between man and man: things inside each man: and relations between man and the power that made him. We can all co-operate in the first one. Disagreements begin with the second and become serious with the third. It is in dealing with the third that the main differences between Chris-

5

tian and non-Christian morality come out. For the rest of these Talks I am going to assume the Christian point of view [1] and look at the whole picture as it will be if Christianity is true.

[1] These Talks will therefore contain no arguments to show that Christianity *is* true. Those who want to know why I think it is true will find what I have to say on that subject in my previous book of broadcast talks, called *The Case for Christianity*.

THE "CARDINAL VIRTUES"— Prudence

Temperance, Justice, Fortitude

IF you are allowed to talk for only ten minutes, pretty well everything else has to be sacrificed to brevity. One of my chief reasons for dividing morality up into three parts (with my picture of the ships sailing in convoy) was that this seemed the shortest way of covering the ground. Here I want to give some idea of another way in which the subject has been divided by old writers, which was too long to use in my Talk, but which is a very good one.

According to this longer scheme there are seven "Virtues." Four of them are called "Cardinal" virtues, and the remaining three are called "Theological" virtues. The "Cardinal" ones are those which all civilised people recognise: the "Theological" are those which, as a rule, only Christians know about. I shall deal with the Theological ones later on: at present I am talking about the four Cardinal virtues. (The word "Cardinal" has nothing to do with "Cardinals" in the Roman Church. It comes from a Latin word meaning "the hinge of a door." These were called "Cardinal" virtues because they are, as we should say, "pivotal.") They are PRUDENCE, TEMPERANCE, JUSTICE, and FORTITUDE.

Prudence means practical commonsense, taking the trouble to think out what you are doing and what is likely to come of it. Nowadays most people hardly think of Prudence as one of the "virtues." In fact, because Christ said we could only get into His world by being like children, many Christians have the idea that, provided you are "good," it doesn't matter being a fool. But that is a misunderstanding. In the first place, most children show plenty of "prudence" about doing the things they are really interested in and think them out quite sensibly. In the second place, as St. Paul points out, Christ never meant that we were to remain children in *intelligence:* on the contrary, He told us to be not only "as harmless as doves," but also "as wise as serpents." He wants a child's heart, but a grown-up's head. He wants us to be simple, single-minded, affectionate, and teachable, as good children are; but He also wants every bit of intelligence we have to be alert at its job, and in first-class fighting trim. The fact that you are giving money to a charity doesn't mean that you needn't try to find out whether that charity is a fraud or not. The fact that what you are thinking about is God Himself (for example, when you are praying), does not mean that you can be content with the same babyish ideas which you had when you were a five-year-old. It is, of course, quite true that God will not love you any the less, or have less use for you, if you happen to have been born with a very second-rate brain. He has room for people with very little sense, but He wants every one to use what sense they have. The proper motto is not "Be good, sweet maid, and let who can be clever," but "Be good, sweet maid, and don't forget that this involves being as clever as you can." God is no fonder of intellectual slackers than of any other slackers. If you are thinking of becoming a Christian, I warn you you are

8

embarking on something which is going to take the whole of you, brains and all. But, fortunately, it works the other way round. Anyone who is honestly trying to be a Christian will soon find his intelligence being sharpened: one of the reasons why it needs no special education to be a Christian is that Christianity is an education itself. That is why an uneducated believer like Bunyan was able to write a book that has astonished the whole world.

Temperance is, unfortunately, one of those words that has changed its meaning. It now usually means teetotalism. But in the days when the second Cardinal virtue was christened "Temperance," it meant nothing of the sort. Temperance referred not specially to drink, but to all pleasures; and it meant not abstaining, but going the right length and no further. It is a mistake to think that Christians ought all to be teetotallers; Mohammedanism, not Christianity, is the teetotal religion. Of course it may be the duty of a particular Christian, or of any Christian, at a particular time, to abstain from strong drink, either because he is the sort of man who can't drink at all without drinking too much, or because he wants to give the money to the poor. But the whole point is that he is abstaining, for a good reason, from something which he does *not* condemn and which he likes to see other people enjoying. One of the marks of a certain type of bad man is that he can't give up a thing himself without wanting every one else to give it up. That isn't the Christian way. An individual Christian may see fit to give up all sorts of things for special reasons—marriage, or meat, or beer, or the cinema; but the moment he starts saying the things are bad in themselves, or looking down his nose at other people who do use them, he has taken the wrong turning.

9

One great piece of mischief has been done by the modern restriction of the word Temperance to the question of drink. It helps people to forget that you can be just as intemperate about lots of other things. A man who makes his golf or his motor bicycle the centre of his life, or a woman who devotes all her thoughts to clothes or bridge or her dog, is being just as "intemperate" as someone who gets drunk every evening. Of course, it doesn't show on the outside so easily: bridge-mania or golf-mania don't make you fall down in the middle of the road. But God doesn't look at outsides.

Justice means much more than the sort of thing that goes on in law courts. It is the old name for everything we should now call "fairness"; it includes honesty, give and take, truthfulness, keeping promises, and all that side of life. And Fortitude includes both kinds of courage— the kind that faces danger as well as the kind that "sticks it" under pain. "Guts" is perhaps the nearest modern English. You will notice, of course, that you can't practise any of the other virtues very long without bringing this one into play.

There is one further point about the Virtues that ought to be noticed. There is a difference between doing some particular just or temperate action and being a just or temperate man. Someone who is not a good tennis player may now and then make a good shot. What you mean by a good player is the man whose eye and muscles and nerves have been so trained by making innumerable good shots that they can now be relied on. They have a certain tone or quality which is there even when he is not playing, just as a mathematician's mind has a certain habit and outlook which is there even when he is not doing mathe-

10

matics. In the same way a man who perseveres in doing just actions gets in the end a certain quality of character. Now it is that quality rather than the particular actions which we mean when we talk of the "virtue" of justice.

This distinction is important for the following reason. If we thought only of the particular actions we might encourage three wrong ideas.

(1) We might think that, provided you did the right thing, it did not matter how or why you did it—whether you did it willingly or unwillingly, sulkily or cheerfully, through fear of public opinion or for its own sake. But the truth is that right actions done for the wrong reason do not help to build the internal quality or character called a "virtue," and it is this quality or character that really matters. (If the bad tennis player hits very hard, not because he sees that a very hard stroke is required, but because he has lost his temper, his stroke might possibly, by luck, help him to win that particular game; but it will not be helping him to become a reliable player.)

(2) We might think that God wanted simply obedience to a set of rules: whereas He really wants *people of a particular sort.*

(3) We might think that the "virtues" were necessary only for this present life—that in the other world we could stop being just because there is nothing to quarrel about and stop being brave because there is no danger. Now it is quite true that there will probably be no occasion for just or courageous acts in the next world, but there will be every occasion for being the sort of people that we can only become as the result of doing such acts here. The point is not that God will refuse you admission to His eternal world if you have not got certain qualities

of character: the point is that if people haven't got at least the beginnings of those qualities inside them, then no possible external conditions could make a "Heaven" for them—that is, could make them happy with the deep, strong, unshakable kind of happiness God intends for us.

III

SOCIAL MORALITY

THE first thing to get clear about Christian morality between man and man is that in this department Christ did not come to preach any brand new morality. The Golden Rule of the New Testament (Do as you would be done by) is a summing up of what every one, at bottom, had always known to be right. Really great moral teachers never do introduce new moralities: it's quacks and cranks who do that. As Dr. Johnson said, "People need to be reminded more often than they need to be instructed." The real job of every moral teacher is to keep on bringing us *back*, time after time, to the old simple principles which we are all so anxious not to see; like bringing a horse back and back to the fence it has refused to jump or bringing a child back and back to the bit in its lesson that it wants to shirk.

The second thing to get clear is that Christianity hasn't got, and doesn't profess to have, a detailed political programme for applying "Do as you would be done by" to a particular society at a particular moment. It couldn't have, of course. It is meant for all men at all times and the particular programme which suited one place or time wouldn't suit another. And, anyhow, that is not how Christianity works. When it tells you to feed the hungry it doesn't give you lessons in cookery. When it tells you to read the Scriptures it doesn't give you lessons in Hebrew and Greek, or even in English grammar. It was never intended to replace or supersede the ordinary human arts and sciences: it is rather a director which will set them all to the right jobs, and a source of energy which will give them all new life, if only they will put themselves at its disposal.

People say, "The Church ought to give us a lead." That is true if they mean it in the right way, but false if they mean it in the wrong way. By the Church they ought to mean the whole body of practising Christians. And when they say that the Church should give us a lead, they ought to mean that some Christians—those who happen to have the right talents—should be economists and statesmen, and that all economists and statesmen should be Christians, and that their whole efforts in politics and economics should be directed to putting "Do as you would be done by" into action. If that happened, and if we others were really ready to take it, then we should find the Christian solution for our own social problems pretty quickly. But, of course, when they ask for a lead from the Church most people mean they want the clergy to put out a political programme. That is silly. The clergy are those particular people within the whole Church who have been specially trained and set aside to look after what concerns us as creatures who are going to live for ever: and we are asking them to do a quite different job for which they have not been trained. The job is really on us, on the laymen. The application of Christian principles, say, to Trades Unionism or education, must come from Christian Trades Unionists and Christian schoolmasters: just as Christian literature comes from Christian novelists and dramatists—not from the bench of Bishops getting together and trying to write plays and novels in their spare time.

All the same, the New Testament, without going into details, gives us a pretty clear hint of what a fully Christian society would be like. Perhaps it gives us more than we can take. It tells us that there are to be no passengers or parasites: if man doesn't work, he oughtn't to eat. Every one is to work with his own hands, and what is more, every one's work is to produce something good: there will be no manufacture of silly luxuries and then of sillier advertisements to persuade us to buy them. And there is to be no "swank" or "side," no putting on airs. To that extent a Christian society would be what we now call Leftist. On the other hand, it is always insisting on obedience—obedience (and outward marks of respect) from all of us to properly appointed magistrates, from children to parents, and (I'm afraid this is going to be very unpopular) from wives to husbands. Thirdly, it is to be a cheerful society: full of singing and rejoicing, and regarding worry or anxiety as wrong. Courtesy is one of the Christian virtues; and the New Testament hates what it calls "busybodies."

If there were such a society in existence and you or I visited it, I think we'd come away with a curious impression. We should feel that its economic life was very socialistic and, in that sense, advanced, but that its family life and its code of manners were rather old fashioned—perhaps even ceremonious and aristocratic. Each of us would like some bits of it, but I'm afraid very few of us would like the whole thing. That is just what one would

15

expect if Christianity is the total plan for the human machine. We have all departed from that total plan in different ways, and each of us wants to make out that his own modification of the original plan is the plan itself. You'll find that again and again about anything that is really Christian: every one is attracted by bits of it and wants to pick out those bits and leave the rest. That is why we don't get much further: and that is why people who are fighting for quite opposite things can both say they're fighting for Christianity.

Now another point. There is one bit of advice given to us by the ancient heathen Greeks, and by the Jews in the Old Testament, and by the great Christian teachers of the Middle Ages, which the modern economic system has completely disobeyed. All these people told us not to lend money at interest: and lending money at interest—what we call investment—is the basis of our whole system. Now it may not absolutely follow that we're wrong. Some people say that when Moses and Aristotle and the Christians agreed in forbidding interest (or "usury" as they called it), they could not foresee the joint stock company, and were only thinking of the private money-lender, and that, therefore, we need not bother about what they said. That is a question I can't decide on. I am not an economist and I simply don't know whether the investment system is responsible for the state we are in or not. This is where we want the Christian economist. But I should not have been honest if I had not told you that three great civilisations had agreed (or so it seems at first sight) in condemning the very thing on which we have based our whole life. — *investment*

One more point and then I'm done. In the passage

16

where the New Testament says that every one must work, it gives as a reason "in order that he may have something to give to those in need." Charity—giving to the poor— is an essential part of Christian morality: in the frightening parable of the sheep and the goats it seems to be the point on which everything turns. Some people nowadays say that charity ought to be unnecessary and that instead of giving to the poor we ought to be producing a society in which there were no poor to give to. Well, they may be quite right in saying that we ought to produce that kind of society. But if anyone thinks that, as a consequence, you can stop giving in the meantime, then he has parted company with all Christian morality. I don't believe one can settle how much we ought to give. I'm afraid the only safe rule is to give more than we can spare.

And now, before I end, I am going to venture on a guess as to how this talk has affected any people who haven't yet switched off. My guess is that there are some Leftist people in the audience who are very angry that it hasn't gone further in that direction, and some people of an opposite sort who are angry because they think it has gone much too far. If so, that brings us right up against the real snag in all this drawing up of blue prints for a Christian society. Most of us are not really approaching the subject in order to find out what Christianity says: we are approaching it in the hope of finding support from Christianity for the views of our own party. We are looking for an ally where we are offered either a Master or—a Judge. I'm just the same. There are bits in this talk that I wanted to leave out. And that is why nothing whatever is going to come of such talks unless we go a much longer way round. A Christian society is not going to arrive until

17

most of us really want it: and we are not going to want it until we become fully Christian. I may repeat, "Do as you would be done by" till I am black in the face, but I can't really carry it out till I love my neighbour as myself: and I can't learn to love my neighbour as myself till I learn to love God: and I can't learn to love God except by learning to obey Him. And so, as I warned you, we are driven on to something more inward—driven on from social matters to religious matters. For the longest way round is the shortest way home.

IV

MORALITY AND PSYCHOANALYSIS

I said last week that we should never get a Christian society unless most of us became Christian individuals. That does not mean, of course, that we can put off doing anything about society until some imaginary date in the far future. It means that we must begin both jobs at once —(1) the job of seeing how "Do as you would be done by" can be applied in detail to modern society, and (2) the job of becoming the sort of people who really would apply it if we saw how. And to-day I want to begin considering what the Christian idea of a good man is—the Christian specification for the human machine.

Before I come down to details there are two more general points I'd like to make. First of all, since Christian morality claims to be a technique for putting the human machine right, I think you would like to know how it is related to another technique which seems to make a similar claim—namely, Psychoanalysis.

Now you want to distinguish very clearly between two things: between the actual medical theories and technique of the psychoanalysts, and the general philosophical view of the world which Freud and some others have gone on to add to this. The second thing—the philosophy of Freud—is in direct contradiction to Christianity: and also in direct contradiction to the other great psychologist, Jung. And furthermore, when Freud is talking about how to cure neurotics he is speaking as a specialist on his own subject, but when he goes on to talk general philosophy he is speaking as an amateur. It is therefore quite sensible to attend to him with respect in the one case and not in the other—and that's what I do. I am all the readier to do it because I've found that when he is talking off his own subject and on a subject I do know something about (namely, languages) he is very ignorant. But psychoanalysis itself, apart from all the philosophical additions that Freud and others have made to it, is not in the least contradictory to Christianity. Its technique overlaps with Christian morality at some points and it wouldn't be a bad thing if every parson knew something about it: but it doesn't run the same course all the way, for the two techniques are doing rather different things.

When a man makes a moral choice two things are involved. One is the act of choosing. The other is the various feelings, impulses and so on which his psychological outfit presents him with, and which are the *raw material* of his choice. Now this raw material may be of two kinds. Either it may be what we would call normal: it may consist of the sort of feelings that are common to all men. Or else it may consist of quite unnatural feelings due to things that have gone wrong in his subconscious. Thus fear of things that are really dangerous would be an example of the first kind: an irrational fear of cats or flies would be an example of the second kind. The desire of a man for a woman would be of the first kind: the perverted desire of a man for a man would be of the second. Now what psychoanalysis undertakes to do is to remove

psychoanalysis — remove abnormal feelings
morality — what to choose.

the abnormal feelings, that is, to give the man better raw material for his acts of choice: morality is concerned with the acts of choice themselves.

Put it this way. Imagine three men who go to a war. One has the ordinary natural fear of danger that any man has and he subdues it by moral effort and becomes a brave man. Let us suppose that the other two have, as a result of things in their subconsciousness, exaggerated, irrational fears, which no amount of moral effort can do anything about. Now suppose that a psychoanalyst comes along and cures these two: that is, he puts them both back in the position of the first man. Well it is just then that the psychoanalytical problem is over and the moral problem begins. Because, now that they are cured, these two men might take quite different lines. The first might say, "Thank goodness I've got rid of all those doo-dahs. Now at last I can do what I always wanted to do—my duty to the cause of freedom." But the other might say, "Well, I'm very glad that I now feel moderately cool under fire, but, of course, that doesn't alter the fact that I'm still jolly well determined to look after Number One and let the other chap do the dangerous job whenever I can. Indeed one of the good things about feeling less frightened is that I can now look after myself much more efficiently and can be much cleverer at hiding the fact from the others." Now this difference is a purely moral one and Psychoanalysis can't do anything about it. However much you improve the man's raw material, you've still got something else: the real, free choice of the man, on the material presented to him, either to put his own advantage first or to put it last. And this free choice is the only thing that morality is concerned with.

The bad psychological material is not a sin but a disease. It doesn't need to be repented of, but to be cured. And by the way, that is very important. Human beings judge one another by their external actions. God judges them by their moral choices. When a neurotic who has a pathological horror of cats forces himself to pick up a cat for some good reason, it is quite possible that in God's eyes he has shown more courage than a healthy man may have shown in winning the V.C. When a man who has been perverted from his youth and taught that cruelty is the right thing, does some tiny little kindness, or refrains from some cruelty he might have committed, and thereby, perhaps, risks being sneered at by his companions, he may, in God's eyes, be doing more than you and I would do if we gave up life itself for a friend.

It is as well to put this the other way round. Some of us who seem quite nice people may, in fact, have made so little use of a good heredity and a good upbringing that we are really worse than those whom we regard as fiends. Can we be quite certain how we should have behaved if we'd been saddled with the psychological outfit, and then with the bad upbringing, and then with the power, say, of Himmler? That is why Christians are told not to judge. We see only the results which a man's choices make out of his raw material. But God doesn't judge him on the raw material at all, but on what he has done with it. Most of the man's psychological make-up is probably due to his body: when his body dies all that will fall off him, and the real central man, the thing that chose, that made the best or the worst out of this material, will stand naked. All sorts of nice things which we thought our own, but which were really due to a good digestion, will fall off

22

actions — choice:

some of us: all sorts of nasty things which were due to complexes or bad health will fall off others. We shall then, for the first time, see every one as he really was. There will be surprises.

And that leads on to my second point. People often think of Christian morality as a kind of bargain in which God says, "If you keep a lot of rules I'll reward you, and if you don't I'll do the other thing." I don't think that is the best way of looking at it. I'd much rather say that every time you make a choice you are turning the central part of you, the part of you that chooses, into something a little different from what it was before. And taking your life as a whole, with all your innumerable choices, all your life long you are slowly turning this central thing either into a heavenly creature or into a hellish creature: either into a creature that is in harmony with God, and with other creatures, and with itself, or else into one that is in a state of war and hatred with God, and with its fellow-creatures, and with itself. To be the one kind of creature *is* heaven: that is, it is joy and peace and knowledge and power. To be the other means madness, horror, idiocy, rage, impotence, and eternal loneliness. Each of us at each moment is progressing to the one state or the other.

That explains what always used to puzzle me about Christian writers; they seem to be so very strict and finicking at one moment and so very free and easy at another. They talk about mere sins of thought as if they were immensely important: and then they talk about the most frightful murders and treacheries as if you'd only got to repent and all would be forgiven. But I've begun to see they are right. What they are always thinking of is the mark which the action leaves on that tiny central self

23

which no one sees in this life but which each of us will have to endure—or enjoy—for ever. One man may be so placed that his anger sheds the blood of thousands, and another so placed that however angry he gets he can't do much damage. But the little mark on the soul may be much the same in both. Each has done something to himself which, unless he repents, will make it harder for him to keep out of the rage next time he's tempted, and will make the rage worse when he does fall into it. Each of them, if he seriously turns to God, can have that twist in the central man straightened out again: each is, in the long run, doomed if he won't. The bigness or smallness of the thing, seen from the outside, are not what really matters.

One last point. Remember that, as I said, the right direction leads not only to peace but to knowledge. When a man is getting better he understands more and more clearly the evil that is still left in him. When a man is getting worse, he understands his own badness less and less. A moderately bad man knows he's not very good: a thoroughly bad man thinks he's all right. This is common-sense, really. You understand sleep when you're awake, not while you're sleeping. You can see mistakes in arithmetic when your mind is working properly: while you're making them you can't see them. Good people know about good *and* evil: bad people don't know about either.

V

SEXUAL MORALITY

To-day I am going to talk about Christian morality as regards sex, what Christians call the virtue of chastity. This is the most unpopular of the Christian virtues. There is no getting away from it: the old Christian rule is, "Either marriage, with complete faithfulness to your partner, or else total abstinence." Now this is so difficult and so contrary to our instincts, that obviously either Christianity is wrong or our sexual instinct, as it now is, has gone wrong. One or the other. Of course, being a Christian, I think it is the instinct which has gone wrong.

But I have other reasons for thinking so. The biological purpose of sex is children, just as the biological purpose of eating is to repair the body. Now if we eat whenever we feel inclined and just as much as we want, it's quite true that most of us will eat too much: but not terrifically too much. One man may eat enough for two, but he doesn't eat enough for ten. The appetite goes a little beyond its biological purpose, but not enormously. But if a healthy young man indulged his sexual appetite whenever he felt inclined, and if each act produced a baby, then in ten years he might easily populate a small village. This appetite is in ludicrous and preposterous excess of its function.

Or take it another way. You can get a large audience together for a strip-tease act—that is, to watch a girl undress on the stage: now suppose you came to a country where you could fill a theatre by simply bringing a covered plate on to the stage and then slowly lifting the cover so as to let every one see, just before the lights went out, that it contained a mutton chop or a bit of bacon, wouldn't you think that in that country something had gone wrong with the appetite for food? And wouldn't anyone who had grown up in a different world think there was something equally queer about the state of the sex instinct among us?

Here's a third point. You find very few people who want to eat things that really aren't food or to do other things with food instead of eating it. In other words, perversions of the food appetite are rare. But perversions of the sex instinct are numerous, hard to cure, and frightful. I am sorry to have to go into all these details, but I must. The reason why I must is that you and I, for the last twenty years, have been fed all day long on good solid lies about sex. We've been told, till one's sick of hearing it, that sexual desire is in the same state as any of our other natural desires and that if only we give up the silly old Victorian idea of hushing it up, everything in the garden will be lovely. It's just not true. The moment you look at the facts, and away from the propaganda, you see that it isn't.

They'll tell you sex has become a mess because it was hushed up. But for the last twenty years it has *not* been hushed up. It has been chattered about all day long. Yet it is still in a mess. If hushing up had been the cause of the trouble, ventilation would have set it right. But it hasn't. I think it is the other way round. I think the human race originally hushed it up because it had become such a mess. Modern people are always saying, "Sex is nothing to be ashamed of." They may mean two things. They may mean, "There is nothing to be ashamed of in the fact that the human race reproduces itself in a certain way, nor in the fact that it gives pleasure." If they mean that, they are right. Christianity says the same. It is not the thing, nor the pleasure, that's the trouble. The old Christian teachers said that if man had never fallen, sexual pleasure, instead of being less than it is now, would actually have been greater. I know some muddle-headed Christians have talked as if Christianity thought that sex, or the body, or pleasure were bad in themselves. But they were wrong. Christianity is almost the only one of the great religions which thoroughly approves of the body—which believes that matter is good, that God Himself once took on a human body, that some kind of body is going to be given to us even in Heaven and is going to be an essential part of our happiness, our beauty, and our energy. Christianity has glorified marriage more than any other religion: and nearly all the greatest love poetry in the world has been produced by Christians. If anyone says that sex, in itself, is bad, Christianity contradicts him at once. But, of course, when people say, "Sex is nothing to be ashamed of," they may mean "the state into which the sexual instinct has now got is nothing to be ashamed of."

If they mean that, I think they are wrong. I think it is everything to be ashamed of. There is nothing to be ashamed of in enjoying your food: there would be everything to be ashamed of if half the world made food the main interest of their lives and spent their time looking at pictures of food and dribbling and smacking their lips. I don't say you and I are individually responsible for the present situation. Our ancestors have handed over to us organisms which are warped in this respect: and we grow up surrounded by propaganda in favour of unchastity. There are people who want to keep our sex instinct inflamed in order to make money out of us. Because, of course, a man with an obsession is a man who has very little sales-resistance. The moral question is, given that situation, what we do about it.

If we really want to be cured, I think we shall be. I mean, if a man tries to go back to the Christian rule, if he makes up his mind either to abstain from sex altogether or to marry one woman and stick to her, he may not completely succeed, especially at first. But as long as he picks himself up each time and starts again as well as he can, he'll be on the right track. He won't damage his central self beyond repair. Those who really want help will get it. The difficulty, of course, is the really wanting it. It is quite easy to think you want something when you don't really. A famous Christian long ago said that when he was a young man he prayed constantly for chastity: but only after several years he came to realise that, while his lips were saying, "Oh, God, make me chaste," his real wishes were secretly adding, "But please don't do it for a few years yet." This catch occurs in prayers on other subjects too.

Now for two final remarks. Don't misunderstand what psychology teaches us about repressions. It teaches us that repressed sex is dangerous. But many people who repeat this don't know that "repression" is a technical term. "Repressing" an impulse does not mean having a conscious desire and resisting it. It means being so frightened of some impulse that you don't let it become conscious at all, so that it goes down into the subconscious and causes trouble. Resisting a conscious desire is quite a different matter, and never did anyone any harm yet. The second remark is this. Although I've had to speak at some length about sex, I want to make it as clear as I possibly can that the centre of Christian morality is not here. If anyone thinks that Christians regard unchastity as *the* great vice, he is quite wrong. The sins of the flesh are bad, but they are the least bad of all sins. All the worst pleasures are purely spiritual: the pleasure of putting other people in the wrong, of bossing and patronising and spoiling sport, and back-biting; the pleasures of power, of hatred. You see, there are two things inside me, competing with the human self which I must try to become. They are the Animal self, and the Diabolical self. The Diabolical self is the worse of the two. That is why a cold, self-righteous prig who goes regularly to Church may be far nearer to hell than a prostitute. But, of course, it is better to be neither.

VI

CHRISTIAN MARRIAGE

THE last Talk was mainly negative. I discussed what was wrong with the sexual impulse in man, but said very little about how it *ought* to work—in other words, about Christian marriage. There are two reasons why I do not particularly want to deal with marriage. The first is that the Christian doctrines on this subject are extremely unpopular. The second is that I have never been married myself, and, therefore, can speak only at second hand. But in spite of that, I feel I can hardly leave the subject out in a series of Talks on Christian morals.

The Christian idea of marriage is based on Christ's words that a man and wife are to be regarded as a single organism—for that is what the words "one flesh" would be in modern English. And the Christians believe that when He said this He was not expressing a sentiment but stating a fact—just as one is stating a fact when one says that a lock and its key are one mechanism, or that a violin and a bow are one musical instrument. The inventor of the human machine was telling us that its two halves, the male and the female, were made to be combined together in pairs, not simply on the sexual level, but totally combined. The monstrosity of sexual intercourse outside marriage is that those who indulge in it are trying to isolate one kind of union (the sexual) from all the other kinds of union which were intended to go along with it and make up the total union. The Christian attitude doesn't mean that there is anything wrong about sexual pleasure, any more than about the pleasure of eating. It means that you mustn't isolate that pleasure and try to get it by itself, any more than you ought to try to get the pleasures of taste without swallowing and digesting, by chewing things and spitting them out again.

As a consequence, Christianity teaches that marriage is for life. There is, of course, a difference here between different Churches: some don't admit divorce at all; some allow it reluctantly in very special cases. It is a great pity that Christians should disagree about such a question; but for an ordinary layman the thing to notice is that the Churches all agree with one another about marriage a great deal more than any of them agrees with the outside world. I mean, they all regard divorce as something like cutting up a living body, as a kind of surgical operation. Some of them think the operation so violent that it can't be done at all; others admit it as a desperate remedy in extreme cases. They are all agreed that it is more like having both your legs cut off than it is like dissolving a business partnership or even deserting a regiment. What they all disagree with is the modern view that it is a simple readjustment of partners, to be made whenever people feel they are no longer in love with one another, or when either of them falls in love with someone else.

Now this is just where misunderstanding arises. People who are defending easy divorce often say, "Surely love is the important thing in marriage." In a sense, yes. Love is the important thing—perhaps the only important thing—in the whole universe. But it depends what you mean by "Love." What most people mean by Love, when they are talking about marriage, is what is called "being in love." Now "being in love" may be a good reason for getting married, though, as far as I can see, it is not a perfect one, for you can fall in love with someone most unsuitable, and even with someone you don't really (in the deeper sense) *like,* or trust. But being in love is not the deeper unity which makes man and wife one organism. I am told (indeed I can see by looking round me) that being in love doesn't last. I don't think it was ever intended to. I think it's a sort of explosion that starts up the engine; it's the pie-crust, not the pie. The real thing, I understand, is something far deeper—something you can live on. I think you can be madly in love with someone you would be sick of after ten weeks: and I'm pretty sure you can be bound heart and soul to someone about whom you don't at that moment feel excited, any more than you feel excited about yourself.

If you disagree with me, of course, you'll say, "He knows nothing about it, he's not married." You may quite possibly be right. But before you say that, do make quite sure that you are judging me by what you really know from your own experience and from watching the lives of your friends, and not by ideas you have derived from novels and films. This is not so easy to do as people think. Our experience is coloured through and through by books and plays and the cinema, and it takes patience and skill to disentangle the things we have really learned from life for ourselves.

One thing people get from books is the idea that if you have married the right person you may expect to go

32

on "being in love" for ever. As a result, when they find they are not, they think this proves they have made a mistake and are entitled to a change—not realising that, when they have changed, the glamour will presently go out of the new love just as it went out of the old one. In this department of life, as in every other, thrills come at the beginning and don't last. The sort of thrill a boy has at the first idea of flying won't go on when he has joined the R.A.F. and is really learning to fly. The thrill you feel on first seeing some delightful place dies away when you really go to live there. Does this mean it would be better not to learn to fly and not to live in the beautiful place? By no means. In both cases, if you go through with it, the dying away of the first thrill will be compensated for by a quieter and more lasting kind of interest. What's more (and I can hardly find words to tell you how important I think this) it is just the people who are ready to submit to the loss of the thrill and settle down to the sober interest, who are then most likely to meet *new* thrills in some quite different direction. The man who has learned to fly and become a good pilot will suddenly discover music; the man who has settled down to live in the beauty-spot will discover gardening.

This is, I think, one little part of what Christ meant by saying that a thing won't really live unless it first dies. It's just no good trying to *keep* any thrill: that's the very worst thing you can do. Let the thrill go—let it die away —go on through that period of death into the quieter interest and happiness that follow—and you'll find you are living in a world of *new* thrills all the time. But if you decide to *live* on thrills and try to prolong them artificially, they will all get weaker and weaker, and fewer and fewer, and you will be a bored, disillusioned old man for the rest of your life. It is because so few people understand this that you find many middle-aged men and women maundering about their lost youth, at the very age when new horizons ought to be appearing and new doors opening all round them. It is so much better fun to learn to swim than to go on endlessly (and hopelessly) trying to get back the feeling you had when you first went paddling as a small boy!

Another notion we get from novels and plays is that "falling in love" is something quite irresistible; something that just happens to one, like measles. And because they believe this, some married people just throw up the sponge and give in when they find themselves attracted by a new acquaintance. But I am inclined to think that these irresistible passions are much rarer in real life than in books, at any rate when one is grown up. When we meet someone beautiful and clever and sympathetic, of course we *ought*, in one sense, to admire and love these good qualities. But is it not very largely in our own choice whether this love shall, or shall not, turn into what we call "being in love"? No doubt, if our minds are chockful of novels and plays and sentimental songs, and our bodies full of alcohol, we shall *turn* any love we feel into that kind of love: just as if you have a rut in your path all the rain-water will run into that rut, and if you wear blue spectacles everything you see will turn blue. But that will be our own fault.

Before leaving the question of divorce, I should like to distinguish two things which are very often confused. The Christian conception of marriage is one: the other is the quite different question—how far Christians, if they are voters or members of Parliament, ought to try to force their views of marriage on the rest of the community by embodying them in the divorce laws. A great many people seem to think that if you are a Christian yourself you should try to make divorce difficult for every one. I don't think that at all. At least I know I'd be very angry if the Mohammedans tried to prevent the rest of us from drinking wine. My own view is that the Churches should frankly recognise that the majority of the British people are not Christians and therefore can't be expected to live Christian lives. There ought to be two distinct kinds of marriage: one governed by the State with rules enforced on all citizens, the other governed by the Church with rules enforced by her on her own members. The distinction ought to be quite sharp, so that a man knows which couples are married in a Christian sense and which are not.

So much for the Christian doctrine about the permanence of marriage. Something else, even more unpopular, remains to be dealt with. Christian wives promise to obey their husbands. In Christian marriage the man is said to be the "head." Two questions obviously arise here. (1) Why should there be a head at all—why not equality? (2) Why should it be the man?

(1) The need for some head follows from the idea that marriage is permanent. Of course, as long as the husband and wife are agreed, no question of a head need arise; and we may hope that this will be the normal state of affairs in a Christian marriage. But when there is a real disagreement, what is to happen? Talk it over, of course; but I am assuming they've done that and still failed to reach agreement. What do they do next? They can't decide by a

majority vote, for in a council of two there can be no majority. Surely, only one or other of two things *can* happen: either they must separate and go their own ways or else one or other of them must have a casting vote. If marriage is permanent, one or other party must, in the last resort, have the power of deciding the family policy. You can't have a permanent association without a constitution.

(2) If there must be a head, why the man? Well, firstly, is there any very serious wish that it should be the woman? As I have said, I'm not married myself, but as far as I can see, even a woman who wants to be the head of her own house does not usually admire the same state of things when she finds it going on next door. She is much more likely to say "Poor Mr. X! Why he allows that appalling woman to boss him about the way she does is more than I can imagine." I don't think she is even very flattered if anyone mentions the fact of her *own* "headship." There must be something unnatural about the rule of wives over husbands, because the wives themselves are half ashamed of it and despise the husbands whom they rule. But there is also another reason; and here I speak quite frankly as a bachelor, because it is a reason you can see from outside even better than from inside. The relations of the family to the outer world —what might be called its foreign policy—must depend, in the last resort, upon the man, because he always ought to be, and usually is, much more just to the outsiders. A woman is primarily fighting for her own children and husband against the rest of the world. Naturally, almost, in a sense, rightly, their claims over-ride, for her, all other claims. She is the special trustee of their

36

interests. The function of the husband is to see that this natural preference of hers isn't given its head. He has the last word in order to protect other people from the intense family patriotism of the wife. If anyone doubts this, let me ask a simple question. If your dog has bitten the child next door, or your child has hurt the dog next door, which would you sooner have to deal with, the master of that house or the mistress? Or, if you are a married woman, let me ask you this question. Much as you admire your husband, would you not say that his chief failing is his tendency not to stick up for his rights and yours against the neighbours as vigorously as you would like? A bit of an Appeaser?

VII

FORGIVENESS

I SAID last week that chastity was the most unpopular of
the Christian virtues. But I am not sure I was right. I
believe the one I have to talk of to-day is even more unpopular: the Christian rule, "Thou shalt love thy neighbour as thyself." Because in Christian morals "thy neighbour" includes "thy enemy," and so we come up against
this terrible duty of forgiving our enemies.

Every one says forgiveness is a lovely idea, until they
have something to forgive, as we have in war-time. And
then, to mention the subject at all is to be greeted with
howls of anger. It isn't that people think this too high
and difficult a virtue: it is that they think it hateful and
contemptible. "That sort of talk makes them sick," they
say. And half of you already want to ask me, "I wonder
how you'd feel about forgiving the Gestapo if you were
a Pole or a Jew?"

So do I. I wonder very much. Just as when Christianity
tells me that I must not deny my religion even to save
myself from death by torture, I wonder very much what
I should do when it came to the point. I am not trying to
tell you in these talks what I could do—I can do precious
little—I am telling you what Christianity is. I didn't in-
vent it. And there, right in the middle of it, I find "For-

give us our sins as we forgive those that sin against us." There is no slightest suggestion that we are offered forgiveness on any other terms. It is made perfectly clear that if we don't forgive we shall not be forgiven. There are no two ways about it. What are we to do?

Well, it is going to be hard enough, anyway, but I think there are two things we can do to make it easier. When you start mathematics you don't begin with the calculus; you begin with simple addition. In the same way, if we really want (but all depends on *really wanting*) to learn how to forgive, perhaps we'd better start with something easier than the Gestapo. One might start with forgiving one's husband or wife, or parents or children, or the nearest N.C.O., for something they've done or said in the last week. That will probably keep us busy for the moment. And secondly, we might try to understand exactly what loving your neighbour as yourself means. I have got to love him as I love myself. Well, how exactly do I love myself?

Now that I come to think of it, I have not exactly got a feeling of fondness or affection for myself, and I don't even always enjoy my own society. So apparently "Love your neighbour" doesn't mean "feel fond of him" or "find him attractive." I ought to have seen that before, because, of course, you can't feel fond of a person, by trying. Do I think well of myself, think myself a nice chap? Well, I'm afraid I sometimes do, but that isn't why I love myself. In fact it is the other way round: my self-love makes me think myself nice, but thinking myself nice isn't why I love myself. So loving my enemies doesn't apparently mean thinking *them* nice either. That is an enormous relief. For a good many people imagine that forgiving your enemies means making out that they are really not such bad fellows after all, when it is quite plain that they are. Go a step further. In my most clear-sighted moments not only do I not think myself a nice man, but I know that I am a very nasty one. I can look at some of the things I have done with horror and loathing. So apparently I am allowed to loathe and hate some of the things my enemies do. Now that I come to think of it, I remember Christian teachers telling me long ago that I must hate a bad man's actions, but not hate the bad man: or, as they would say, hate the sin but not the sinner.

For a long time I used to think this a silly, straw-splitting distinction: how could you hate what a man did and not hate the man? But years later it occurred to me that there was one man to whom I had been doing this all my life—namely myself. However much I might dislike my own cowardice or conceit or greed, I went on loving myself. There had never been the slightest difficulty about it. In fact the very reason why I hated these things was that I loved the man. Just because I loved myself, I was sorry to find that I was the sort of man who did those things. Consequently, Christianity does not want us to reduce by one atom the hatred we feel for cruelty and treachery. We ought to hate them. Not one word of what we have said about them needs to be unsaid. But it does want us to hate them in the same way in which we hate things in ourselves: being sorry that the man should have done such things, and hoping, if it is anyway possible, that somehow, sometime, somewhere, he can be cured and made human again.

The real test is this. Suppose one reads a story of filthy atrocities in the paper. Then suppose that something

40

turns up suggesting that the story might not be quite true, or not quite so bad as it was made out. Is one's first feeling, "Thank God, even they aren't quite such devils as that," or is it a feeling of disappointment, and even a determination to cling to the first story for the sheer pleasure of thinking your enemies as bad as possible? If it is the second then it is, I'm afraid, the first step in a process which, if followed to the end, will make us into devils. You see, one is beginning to wish that black was a little blacker. If we give that wish its head, later on we shall wish to see grey as black, and then to see white itself as black. Finally, we shall insist on seeing everything, God and our friends and ourselves included, as bad, and not be able to stop doing it: we shall be fixed for ever in a universe of pure hatred.

Now a step further. Does loving your enemy mean not punishing him? No, for loving myself does not mean that I ought not to subject myself to punishment—even to death. If one had committed a murder, the right Christian thing to do would be to give yourself up to the police and be hanged. It is, therefore, in my opinion, perfectly right for a Christian judge to sentence a man to death or a Christian soldier to kill an enemy. I always have thought so, ever since I became a Christian, and long before the war. There's no good quoting "Thou shalt not kill." There are two Greek words: the ordinary word to *kill* and the word to *murder*. And when Christ quotes that commandment He uses the *murder* one in all three accounts, Matthew, Mark, and Luke. And I am told there is the same distinction in Hebrew. All killing is not murder any more than all sexual intercourse is adultery. When soldiers came to St. John the Baptist asking what to do, he never remotely suggested that they ought to leave the army: nor did Christ when He met a Roman sergeant-major—what they called a centurion. The idea of the knight—the Christian in arms for the defence of a good cause—is one of the great Christian ideas. War is a dreadful thing, and I can respect an honest pacifist, though I think he is entirely mistaken. What I cannot understand is this sort of half pacifism you get nowadays which gives people the idea that though you have got to fight, you ought to do it with a long face and as if you were ashamed of it. It is that feeling that robs lots of magnificent young Christians in the Services of something they have a right to, something which is the natural accompaniment of courage—a kind of gaiety and whole-heartedness. But I must get back to my subject.

I imagine somebody will say, "Well, if one is allowed to condemn the enemy's acts, and punish him, and kill him, what difference is left between Christian morality and the ordinary view?" All the difference in the world. Remember, we Christians think man lives for ever. Therefore, what really matters is those little marks or twists on the central, inside part of the soul which are going to turn it, in the long run, into a heavenly or a hellish creature. We may kill if necessary, but we musn't hate and enjoy hating. We may punish if necessary, but we mustn't enjoy it. In other words, something inside us, the feeling of resentment, the feeling that wants to get one's own back, must be simply killed. I don't mean that anyone can decide to-night that he won't feel it any more. That is not how things happen. I mean that every time it bobs its head up, day after day, year after year, all our lives long, we've just got to hit it on the head. It is hard work, but the attempt is not impossible. Even while we kill and punish we must try to feel about the enemy as we feel about ourselves—to wish that he were not bad, to hope that he may, in this world or another, be cured: in fact, to wish his good. That is what is meant in the Bible by loving him: wishing his good, not feeling fond of him nor saying he's nice when he isn't.

I admit that this means loving people who have nothing lovable about them. But then, has oneself anything lovable about it? You love it simply because it *is* yourself. God intends us to love all selves in the same way and for the same reason: only He's given us the sum ready worked out in our own case to show us how it works. We have then to go on and apply the rule to all the other selves. Perhaps it makes it easier if we remember that that is how He loves us. Not for any nice, attractive qualities we think we have, but just because we are the things called selves. For really there is nothing else in us to love: creatures like us who actually find hatred such a pleasure that to give it up is like giving up beer or tobacco. . . .

VIII

THE GREAT SIN

To-day I come to that part of Christian morals where they differ most sharply from all other morals. There is one vice of which no man in the world is free; which every one in the world simply loathes when he sees it in someone else; and of which hardly any people, except Christians, ever imagine that they are guilty themselves. I have heard people admit that they are bad-tempered, or that they can't keep their heads about girls or drink, or even that they are cowards. I don't think I have ever heard anyone who was not a Christian accuse himself of this vice. And at the same time I have very seldom met anyone, who was not a Christian, who showed the slightest mercy to it in others. There is no fault which makes a man more unpopular, and no fault which we are more unconscious of in ourselves. And the more we have it ourselves, the more we dislike it in others.

The vice I am talking of is Pride or Self-Conceit: and the virtue opposite to it, in Christian morals, is called Humility. You may remember, when I was talking about sexual morality, I warned you that the centre of Christian morals did not lie there. Well, now, we have come to the centre. According to Christian teachers, the essential vice, the utmost evil, is Pride. Unchastity, anger, greed,

44

drunkenness, and all that, are mere flea-bites in comparison: it was through Pride that the devil became the devil: Pride leads to every other vice: it is the complete anti-God state of mind.

Does this seem to you exaggerated? If so, think it over. I pointed out a moment ago that the more pride one had, the more one disliked pride in others. In fact, if you want to find out how proud you are the easiest way is to ask yourself, "How much do I dislike it when other people snub me, or refuse to take any notice of me, or shove their oar in, or patronise me, or show off?" The point is that each person's pride is in competition with every one else's pride. It is because I wanted to be the big noise at the party that I am so annoyed at someone else being the big noise. Two of a trade never agree. Now what you want to get clear is that Pride is *essentially* competitive—is competitive by its very nature—while the other vices are competitive only, so to speak, by accident. Pride gets no pleasure out of having something, only out of having more of it than the next man. We say that people are proud of being rich, or clever, or good looking, but they are not. They are proud of being richer, or cleverer, or better looking than others. If every one else became equally rich, or clever, or good looking there'd be nothing to be proud about. It's the comparison that makes you proud: the pleasure of being above the rest. Once the element of competition has gone, pride has gone. That is why I say that Pride is essentially competitive in a way the other vices are not. The sexual impulse *may* drive two men into competition if they both want the same girl. But that is only by accident; they might just as likely have wanted two different girls. But a proud man

45

will take your girl from you, not because he wants her, but just to prove to himself that he's a better man than you. Greed *may* drive men into competition, if there isn't enough to go round; but the proud man, even when he's got more than he can possibly want, will try to get still more just to assert his power. Nearly all those evils in the world which people put down to greed or selfishness are really far more the result of Pride.

Take it with money. Greed will certainly make a man want money, for the sake of a better house, better holidays, better things to eat and drink. But only up to a point. What is it that makes a man with £10,000 a year anxious to get £20,000 a year? It is not the greed for more pleasure. £10,000 will give all the luxuries that any man can really enjoy. It is Pride—the wish to be richer than some other rich man, and (still more) the wish for power. For, of course, power is what Pride really enjoys: there is nothing makes a man feel so superior to others as being able to move them about like toy soldiers. What makes a pretty girl spread misery wherever she goes by collecting admirers? Certainly not her sexual instinct: that kind of girl is quite often sexually frigid. It is Pride. What is it that makes a political leader or a whole nation go on and on, demanding more and more? Pride again. Pride is competitive by its very nature: that is why it goes on and on. If I am a proud man, then, as long as there is one man in the whole world more powerful, or richer, or cleverer than I, he is my rival and my enemy.

The Christians are right: it is Pride which has been the chief cause of misery in every nation and every family since the world began. Other vices may sometimes bring people together: you may find good fellowship and jokes and friendliness among drunken people or unchaste people. But Pride always means enmity—it *is* enmity. And not only enmity between man and man, but enmity to God.

In God you come up against something which is in every respect immeasurably superior to yourself. Unless you know God as that—and therefore know yourself as nothing in comparison—you can't know God at all. As long as you are proud you can't know God at all. A proud man is always looking down on things and people: and, of course, as long as you're looking down, you can't see something that's above you.

That raises a terrible question. How is it that people who are quite obviously eaten up with Pride can *say* they believe in God and appear to themselves very religious? I'm afraid it means they are worshipping an imaginary God. They theoretically admit themselves to be nothing in the presence of this phantom God, but are really all the time imagining how He approves of them and thinks them far better than ordinary people: that is, they pay a pennyworth of imaginary humility to Him and get out of it a pound's worth of Pride towards their fellow-men. I suppose it was of those people Christ was thinking when He said that some would preach about Him and cast out devils in His name, only to be told at the end of the world that He had never known them. And any of us may at any moment be in this death-trap. Luckily, we have a test. Whenever we find that our religious life is making us feel that we are good—above all, that we are better than someone else—I think we may be sure that we are being acted on, not by God, but by the devil. The real test of being in the presence of God is that you either forget about yourself altogether or see yourself as a small, dirty object.

It is a terrible thing that the worst of all the vices can smuggle itself into the very centre of our religious life. But you can see why. The other, and less bad, vices come from the devil working on us through our animal nature. But this doesn't come through our animal nature at all. It comes *direct* from Hell. It is purely spiritual: consequently it is far more subtle and deadly. For the same reason, Pride can often be used to beat down the simpler vices. Teachers, in fact, often appeal to a boy's Pride, or, as they call it, his self-respect, to make him behave decently: many a man has overcome cowardice, or lust, or ill-temper by learning to think that they are beneath his dignity—that is, by Pride. The devil laughs. He's perfectly content to see you becoming chaste and brave and self-controlled provided, all the time, he is setting up in you the Dictatorship of Pride—just as he'd be quite content to cure your chilblains if he was allowed, in return, to give you cancer. For Pride *is* spiritual cancer: it eats up the very possibility of love, or contentment, or even commonsense.

Before finishing, I want to guard against two misunderstandings. First of all, don't think Pride is something God forbids because He is offended at it, or that Humility is something He demands as due to His own dignity—as if God Himself was proud. He is not in the least worried about His dignity. The point is, He wants you to know Him: wants to give you Himself. And He and you are two things of such a kind that if you really get into any kind of touch with Him you will, in fact, be humble—delightedly humble, feeling the infinite relief

48

of having for once got rid of all the silly nonsense about *your* dignity which has made you restless and unhappy all your life. He is trying to make you humble in order to make this moment possible: trying to take off a lot of silly, ugly fancy-dress in which we have all got ourselves up and are strutting about like the little idiots we are. I wish I had got a bit further with humility myself: if I had, I could probably tell you more about the relief, the comfort, of taking the fancy-dress off—getting rid of the false self, with all its "Look at me" and "Aren't I a good boy?" and all its posing and posturing. To get even near it, even for a moment, is like a drink of cold water to a man in a desert.

The second point is this. Don't imagine that if you meet a really humble man he will be what most people call "humble" nowadays: he won't be a sort of greasy, smarmy person, who's always telling you that, of course, he's nobody. Probably all you'll think about him is that he seemed a cheerful, intelligent chap who took a real interest in what *you* said to *him*. If you *do* dislike him it will be because you feel a little envious of anyone who seems to enjoy life so easily. He won't be thinking about humility: he won't be thinking about himself at all. There I must stop. If anyone would like to acquire humility, I can, I think, tell him the first step. The first step is to realise that one is proud. And a biggish step, too. At least, nothing whatever can be done before it. If you think you're not conceited, it means you are very conceited indeed.

49

IX

CHARITY

I SAID in an earlier Talk that there were four "Cardinal" virtues and three "Theological" virtues. The three Theological ones are Faith, Hope, and Charity. Faith is going to be dealt with in the last two Talks. Charity was partly dealt with in No. VIII, but as I had only ten minutes I had to concentrate on that part of Charity which is called Forgiveness. I now want to add a little more.

First, as to the meaning of the word. "Charity" now means simply what used to be called "alms"—that is, giving to the poor. Originally it had a much wider meaning. (You can see how it got the modern sense. If a man has "charity," giving to the poor is one of the most *obvious* things he does, and so people come to talk as if that were the whole of charity. In the same way, "rhyme" is the most *obvious* thing about poetry, and so people come to mean by "poetry" simply rhyme and nothing more.) Charity means "Love, in the Christian sense." But love, in the Christian sense, does not mean an emotion. It is a state not of the feelings but of the will; that state of the will which we have *naturally* about ourselves, and must *learn* to have about other people.

I pointed out in the Talk on Forgiveness that our love for ourselves does not mean that we *like* ourselves. It means that we wish our own good. In the same way Christian Love (or Charity) for our neighbours is quite a different thing from liking or affection. We "like" or are "fond of" some people, and not of others. It is important to understand that this natural "liking" is neither a sin nor a virtue, any more than your likes and dislikes in food are a sin or a virtue. It is just a fact. But, of course, what we do about it is either sinful or virtuous.

Natural liking or affection for people makes it easier to be "charitable" towards them. It is, therefore, normally a duty to encourage our affections—to "like" people as much as we can (just as it is often our duty to encourage our liking for exercise or wholesome food)—not because this liking is itself the virtue of charity, but because it is a help to it. On the other hand, it is also necessary to keep a very sharp look-out for fear our liking for some one person makes us uncharitable, or even unfair, to someone else. There are even cases where our liking conflicts with our charity towards the person we like. For example, a doting mother may be tempted by natural affection to "spoil" her child; that is, to gratify her own affectionate impulses at the expense of the child's real happiness later on.

But though natural likings should normally be encouraged, it would be quite wrong to think that the way to become charitable is to sit trying to manufacture affectionate feelings. Some people are "cold" by temperament; that may be a misfortune for them, but it is no more a sin than having a bad digestion is a sin; and it does not cut them out from the chance, or excuse them from the duty, of learning charity. The rule for all of us is perfectly simple. Don't waste time bothering whether you "love" your neighbour; act *as if you did*. As soon as we do this we find one of the great secrets. When you are behaving *as if* you loved someone, you will presently come to love him. If you injure someone you dislike, you will find yourself disliking him more. If you do him a good turn, you will find yourself disliking him less. There is, indeed, one exception. If you do him a good turn, not to please God and obey the law of charity, but to show him what a fine forgiving chap you are, and to put him in your debt, and then sit down to wait for his "gratitude," you will probably be disappointed. (People aren't fools: they have a very quick eye for anything like showing off, or patronage.) But whenever we do good to another self, just because it is a self, made (like us) by God, and desiring its own happiness as we desire ours, we shall have learned to love it a little more or, at least, to dislike it less.

Consequently, though Christian charity sounds a very cold thing to people whose heads are full of sentimentality, and though it is quite distinct from affection, yet it *leads to* affection. The difference between a Christian and a worldly man is not that the worldly man has only affections or "likings" and the Christian has only "charity." The worldly man treats certain people kindly because he "likes" them: the Christian, trying to treat every one kindly, finds himself liking more and more people as he goes on—including people he could not even have imagined himself liking at the beginning.

This same spiritual law works terribly in the opposite direction. The Germans, perhaps, at first ill-treated the Jews because they hated them: they now hate them much more because they have ill-treated them. The more cruel you are, the more you will hate; and the more you hate, the more cruel you will become—and so on in a vicious circle for ever.

Good and evil both increase *at compound interest*. That is why the little decisions you and I make every day are of such infinite importance. The smallest good act to-day is the capture of a strategic point from which, a few months later, you may be able to go on to victories you never dreamed of. An apparently trivial indulgence in lust or anger to-day is the loss of a ridge or railway line or bridgehead from which the enemy may launch an attack otherwise impossible.

Some writers use the word charity to describe not only Christian love between human beings, but also God's love for man and man's love for God. About the second of these two, people are often worried. They are told they ought to love God. They cannot find any such feeling in themselves. What are they to do? The answer is the same as before. Act *as if you did*. Don't sit trying to manufacture feelings. Ask yourself, "If I *were* sure that I loved God, what would I do?" When you have found the answer, go and do it.

On the whole, God's love for us is a much safer subject to think about than our love for Him. Nobody can always have devout feelings: and even if we could, feelings are not what God principally cares about. Christian Love, either towards God or towards man, is an affair of the will. If we are trying to do His will we are obeying the commandment, "Thou shalt love the Lord thy God." He will give us *feelings* of love if He pleases. We cannot create them for ourselves, and we must not demand them as a right. But the great thing to remember is that,

53

though our feelings come and go, His love for us does not. It is not wearied by our sins or our indifference; and, therefore, it is quite relentless in its determination that we shall be cured of those sins, at whatever cost to us, at whatever cost to Him.

X

HOPE

HOPE is one of the Theological virtues. This means that a continual looking forward to the eternal world is not (as some modern people think) a form of escapism or wishful thinking, but one of the things a Christian is meant to do. It does not mean that we are to leave the present world as it is. If you read history you will find that the Christians who did most for the present world were just those who thought most of the next. The Apostles themselves, who set on foot the conversion of the Roman Empire, the great men who built up the Middle Ages, the English Evangelicals who abolished the Slave Trade, all left their mark on Earth, precisely because their minds were occupied with Heaven. It is since Christians have largely ceased to think of the other world that they have become so ineffective in this. Aim at Heaven and you will get earth "thrown in": aim at earth and you will get neither. It seems a strange rule, but something like it can be seen at work in other matters. Health is a great blessing, but the moment you make health one of your main, direct objects you start becoming a crank and imagining there is something wrong with you. You are only likely to get health provided you want other things *more*—food, games, work, fun, open air. In the same way, we shall never save civilisation as long as civilisation is our main object. We must learn to want something else even more.

Most of us find it very difficult to want "Heaven" at all —except in so far as "Heaven" means meeting again our friends who have died. One reason for this difficulty is that we have not been trained: our whole education tends to fix our minds on this world. Another reason is that when the real want for Heaven is present in us, we do not recognise it. Most people, if they had really learned to look into their own hearts, would know that they do want, and want acutely, something that cannot be had in this world. There are all sorts of things in this world that *offer* to give it to you, but they never quite keep their promise. The longings which arise in us when we first fall in love, or first think of some foreign country, or first take up some subject that excites us, are longings which no marriage, no travel, no learning, can really satisfy. I am not now speaking of what would be ordinarily called unsuccessful marriages, or holidays, or learned careers. I am speaking of the best possible ones. There was something we grasped at, in that first moment of longing, which just fades away in the reality. I think every one knows what I mean. The wife may be a good wife, and the hotels and scenery may have been excellent, and chemistry may be a very interesting job: but *something* has evaded us. Now there are two wrong ways of dealing with this fact, and one right way.

(1) The Fool's Way.—He puts the blame on the things themselves. He goes on all his life thinking that if only he tried another woman, or went for a more expensive holiday, or whatever it is, then, this time, he really would catch the mysterious something we are all after. Most of

the bored, discontented, rich people in the world are of this type. They spend their whole lives trotting from woman to woman (through the divorce courts), from continent to continent, from hobby to hobby, always thinking that the latest is "the Real Thing" at last, and always disappointed.

(2) The Way of the Disillusioned "Sensible Man."— He soon decides that the whole thing was moonshine. "Of course," he says, "one feels like that when one's young. But by the time you get to my age you've given up chasing the rainbow's end." And so he settles down and learns not to expect too much and represses the part of himself which used, as he would say, "to cry for the moon." This is, of course, a much better way than the first, and makes a man much happier, and less of a nuisance to society. It tends to make him a prig (he is apt to be rather superior towards what he calls "adolescents"), but, on the whole, he rubs along fairly comfortably. It would be the best line we could take if man didn't live for ever. But supposing infinite happiness really is there, waiting for us? Supposing one *can* really reach the rainbow's end? In that case it would be a pity to find out too late (a moment after death) that by our supposed "commonsense" we had stifled in ourselves the faculty of enjoying it.

(3) The Christian Way.—The Christian says, "Creatures are not born with desires unless satisfaction for those desires exist. A baby feels hunger: well, there is such a thing as food. A duckling wants to swim: well, there is such a thing as water. Men feel sexual desire: well, there is such a thing as sex. If I find in myself a desire which no experience in this world can satisfy, the

most probable explanation is that I was made for another world. If none of my earthly pleasures satisfy it, that does not prove that the universe is a fraud. Probably earthly pleasures were never *meant* to satisfy it, but only to arouse it, to suggest the real thing. If that is so, I must take care, on the one hand, never to despise, or be unthankful for, these earthly blessings, and on the other, never to mistake them for the something else of which they are only a kind of copy, or echo, or mirage. I must keep alive in myself the desire for my true country, which I shall not find till after death; I must never let it get snowed under or turned aside; I must make it the main object of life to press on to that other country and to help others to do the same."

NOTE.—There is no need to be worried by facetious people who try to make the Christian hope of "Heaven" ridiculous by saying they don't want "to spend eternity playing harps." The answer to such people is that if they cannot understand books written for grown-ups, they should not talk about them. All the scriptural imagery (harps, crowns, gold, etc.) is, of course, a merely symbolical attempt to express the inexpressible. Musical instruments are mentioned because for many people (not all) music is the thing known in the present life which most strongly suggests ecstasy and infinity. Crowns are mentioned to suggest the fact that those who are united with God in eternity share His splendour and power and joy. Gold is mentioned to suggest the timelessness of Heaven (gold does not rust) and the preciousness of it. People who take these symbols literally might as well think that when Christ told us to be like doves, He meant that we were to lay eggs!

XI

FAITH

I AM going to talk to-day about what the Christians call Faith. Roughly speaking, the word Faith seems to be used by Christians in two senses or on two levels, and I will take them in turn. In the first sense it means simply Belief—accepting or regarding as true the doctrines of Christianity. That is fairly simple. But what does puzzle people—at least it used to puzzle me—is the fact that Christians regard faith in this sense as a virtue. I used to ask how on earth it can be a virtue—what is there moral or immoral about believing or not believing a set of statements? Obviously, I used to say, a sane man accepts or rejects any statement, not because he wants to or doesn't want to, but because the evidence seems to him good or bad. If he were mistaken about the goodness or badness of the evidence that would not mean he was a bad man, but only that he was not very clever. And if he thought the evidence bad but tried to force himself to believe in spite of it, that would be merely stupid.

Well, I think I still take that view. But what I did not see then—and a good many people do not see still—was this. I was assuming that if the human mind once accepts a thing as true it will automatically go on regarding it as true, until some real reason for reconsidering it turns up.

In fact, I was assuming that the human mind is completely ruled by reason. But that is not so. For example, my reason is perfectly convinced by good evidence that anaesthetics don't smother me and that properly trained surgeons don't start operating until I am unconscious. But that doesn't alter the fact that when they've got me down on the table and clapped their horrible mask over my face, a mere childish panic begins inside me. I start thinking I am going to choke, and I am afraid they will start cutting me up before I am properly over. In other words, I lose my faith in anaesthetics. It is not reason that is taking away my faith: on the contrary, my faith is based on reason. It is my imagination and emotions. The battle is between faith and reason on one side and emotion and imagination on the other.

When you think of it you will see lots of instances of this. A man knows, on perfectly good evidence, that a pretty girl of his acquaintance is a liar and can't keep a secret and ought not to be trusted; but when he finds himself with her his mind loses its faith in that bit of knowledge and he starts thinking, "Perhaps she'll be different this time," and once more makes a fool of himself and tells her something he ought not to have told her. His senses and emotions have destroyed his faith in what he really knows to be true. Or take a boy learning to swim. His reason knows perfectly well that an unsupported human body will not necessarily sink in water: he has seen dozens of people float and swim. But the whole question is whether he will be able to go on believing this when the instructor takes away his hand and leaves *him* unsupported in the water—or whether he will suddenly cease to believe it and get in a fright and go down?

Now just the same thing happens about Christianity. I am not asking anyone to accept Christianity if his best reasoning tells him that the weight of the evidence is against it. That is not the point at which Faith comes in. But supposing a man's reason once decides that the weight of the evidence is for it. I can tell that man what is going to happen to him in the next few weeks. There will come a moment when the news is bad, or he is in trouble, or is living among a lot of other people who don't believe it, and all at once his emotions will rise up and just carry out a sort of blitz on his belief. Or else there will come a moment when he wants a woman, or wants to tell a lie, or feels very pleased with himself, or sees a chance of making a little money in some way that's not perfectly fair: some moment, in fact, at which it would be very convenient if Christianity were *not* true. And once again his wishes and desires will carry out a blitz. I am not talking of moments at which any real new *reasons* against Christianity turn up. Those have to be faced and that is a different matter. I am talking about moments when a mere mood rises up against it.

Now Faith, in the sense in which I am here using the word, is the art of holding on to things your reason has once accepted, in spite of your changing moods. For moods will change, whatever view your reason takes. I know that by experience. Now that I am a Christian I do have moods in which the whole thing looks very unlikely: but when I was an atheist I had moods in which Christianity looked terribly probable. This rebellion of your moods against your real self is going to come anyway. That is why Faith is such a necessary virtue: unless you teach your moods "where they get off," you can never be

61

either a sound Christian or even a sound atheist, but just a creature dithering to and fro, with its beliefs really dependent on the weather and the state of its digestion. Consequently one must train the habit of Faith.

The first step is to recognise the fact that you *have* moods. The next is to make sure that, if you have once accepted Christianity, then some of its main doctrines shall be deliberately held before your mind for some time every day. That is why daily prayers and religious reading and church-going are necessary parts of the Christian life. We have to be continually reminded of what we believe. Neither this belief nor any other will automatically remain alive in the mind. It must be fed. And as a matter of fact, if you examined a hundred people who had lost their faith in Christianity, I wonder how many of them would turn out to have been reasoned out of it by honest argument? Don't most people simply *drift* away?

Now I must turn to Faith in the second or higher sense: and this is the most difficult thing I have tackled yet. I want to approach it by going back to the subject of Humility. You may remember I said that the first step towards humility was to realise that one is proud. I want to add now that the next step is to make some serious attempt to practise the Christian virtues. A week won't do. Things often go swimmingly for the first week. Try six weeks. By that time, having, as far as one can see, fallen back completely or even fallen lower than the point one began from, one will have discovered some truths about oneself. No man knows how bad he is till he has tried very hard to be good. There is a silly idea about, that good people don't know what temptation means.

This is an obvious lie. Only those who try to resist temptation know how strong it is. After all, you find out the strength of the German army by fighting against it, not by giving in. You find out the strength of a wind by trying to walk against it, not by lying down. A man who gives in to temptation after five minutes simply doesn't know what it would have been like an hour later. That is why bad people, in one sense, know very little about badness. They've lived a sheltered life by always giving in. We never find out the strength of the evil impulse inside us until we try to fight it: and Christ, because He was the only man who never yielded to temptation, is also the only man who knows to the full what temptation means—the only complete realist. Very well, then. The main thing we learn from a serious attempt to practise the Christian virtues is that we fail. If there was any idea that God had set us a sort of exam. and that we might get good marks by deserving them, that has to be wiped out. If there was any idea of a sort of bargain—any idea that we could perform our side of the contract and thus put God in our debt so that it was up to Him, in mere justice, to perform His side, that has to be wiped out.

I think every one who has some vague belief in God, until he becomes a Christian, has the idea of an exam. or of a bargain in his mind. The first result of real Christianity is to blow that idea into bits. When they find it blown into bits, some people think this means that Christianity is a failure and give up. They seem to imagine that God is very simple-minded! In fact, of course, He knows all about this. One of the very things Christianity was designed to do was to blow this idea to bits. God has been waiting for the moment at which you discover that there is no question of earning a pass mark in this exam. or putting Him in your debt.

And soon comes another discovery. Every faculty you have, your power of thinking or of moving your limbs from moment to moment, is given you by Him. If you devoted every moment of your whole life exclusively to His service you couldn't give Him anything that wasn't in a sense His own already. So that when we talk of a man doing anything for God or giving anything to God, I will tell you what it is really like. It is like a small child going to its father and saying, "Daddy, give *me* sixpence to buy *you* a birthday present." Of course, the father does, and he is pleased with the child's present. It's all very nice and proper, but only an idiot would think that the father is sixpence to the good on the transaction. When a man has made these two discoveries God can really get to work. It is after this that real life begins. The man is awake now. We can now go on to talk of Faith in the second sense.

XII

FAITH

I want to start by saying something that I would like every one to notice carefully. It is this. If to-day's Talk means nothing to you, if it seems to be trying to answer questions you never asked, drop it at once. Don't bother about it at all. There are certain things in Christianity that can be understood from the outside, before you've become a Christian. But there are a great many things that cannot be understood until after you have got a certain distance along the Christian road. These things are purely practical, though they don't look as if they were. They are directions for dealing with particular cross-roads and obstacles on the journey and they just don't make sense until a man has reached those places. Whenever you find any statement in Christian writings which you can make nothing of, don't worry. Leave it alone. There will come a day, perhaps years later, when you suddenly see what it meant. If one *could* understand it now, it would only do one harm.

Of course all this tells against me as much as anyone else. The thing I am going to try to explain to-day may be ahead of me. I may be thinking I have got there when I haven't. I can only ask instructed Christians to watch very carefully, and tell me when I go wrong; and others to take what I say with a grain of salt—as something offered, because it *may* be a help, not because I am certain I'm right.

I am trying to talk about Faith in the second sense, the higher sense. I said last week that the question of Faith in this sense arises after a man has tried his level best to practise the Christian virtues, and found that he fails, and seen that even if he could he would only be giving back to God what was already God's own. In other words, he discovers his bankruptcy. Now what God cares about, I think, is not exactly our actions. What He cares about is that we should be creatures of a certain kind or quality— the kind of creatures He intended us to be—creatures related to Himself in a certain way. I don't add "and related to one another in a certain way," because that is included: if you are right with Him you will inevitably be right with all your fellow-creatures, just as if all the spokes of a wheel are fitted rightly into the hub and the rim they're bound to be in the right positions to one another. And as long as a man is thinking of God as an examiner who has set him a sort of paper to do, or as the opposite party in a sort of bargain—as long as he is thinking of claims and counter-claims between himself and God—he is not yet in the right relation to Him. He is misunderstanding what he is and what God is. And he cannot get into the right relation until he has discovered the fact of our bankruptcy.

When I say "discovered," I mean *really* discovered: not simply said it parrot fashion. Of course any child, if given a certain kind of religious education, will soon learn to *say* that we have nothing to offer to God that isn't already His own and that we find ourselves failing to offer even that without keeping something back. But I am talking of really discovering this: really finding out by experience that it is true.

Now we cannot, in that sense, discover our failure to keep God's law except by trying our very hardest (and then failing). Unless we really try, whatever we say there will always be at the back of our minds the idea that if we try harder next time we shall succeed in being completely good. Thus, in one sense, the road back to God is a road of moral effort, of trying harder and harder. But in another sense it is not trying that is ever going to bring us home. All this trying leads up to the vital moment at which you turn to God and say, "You must do this. I can't." Don't for Heaven's sake start asking yourselves, "Have I reached that moment?" and don't sit down and start watching your own mind to see if it is coming along. That puts a man quite on the wrong track. When the most important things in our life happen we quite often don't know, at the moment, what is going on. A man doesn't always say to himself, "Hullo! I'm growing up." It is often only when he looks back that he realises what has happened and recognises it as what people call "growing up." You can see it even in simpler matters. A man who starts anxiously watching to see whether he is going to sleep is very likely to remain wide awake. As well, the thing I am talking of now may not happen to every one in a sudden flash—as it did to St. Paul or Bunyan: it may be so gradual that no one could ever point to a particular hour or even a particular year. And what matters is the nature of the change in itself, not how we feel while it is happening. It is the change from being confident about our own efforts to the state in which we despair of doing anything for ourselves and leave it to God.

I know the words "leave it to God" can be misunderstood, but they must stay for the moment. The sense in which a Christian leaves it to God is that he puts all his trust in Christ: trusts that Christ will somehow share with him the perfect human obedience which He carried out from His birth to His crucifixion: that Christ will make the man more like Himself and, in a sense, make good his deficiencies. If you like to put it that way, Christ offers something for nothing: He even offers everything for nothing. In a sense, the whole Christian life consists in accepting that very remarkable offer. But the difficulty is to reach the point of recognising that all we have done and can do is nothing. What we should have liked would be for God to count our good points and ignore our bad ones. Again, in a sense, you may say that no temptation is ever overcome until we stop trying to overcome it—throw up the sponge. But then you couldn't "stop trying" in the right way and for the right reason until you had tried your very hardest. And, in yet another sense, handing everything over to Christ doesn't, of course, mean that you stop trying. To trust Him means, of course, trying to do all that He says. There would be no sense in saying you trusted a person if you didn't take his advice. Thus if you have really handed yourself over to Him, it *must* follow that you are trying to obey Him. But trying in a new way, a less worried way. Not doing these things in order to be saved, but because He has begun to save you already. Not hoping to get to Heaven as a reward for your actions, but inevitably wanting to act in a certain way because a first faint gleam of Heaven is already inside you.

Christians have often disputed as to whether what

leads the Christian home is good actions, or Faith in Christ. I have no right really to speak on such a difficult question, but it does seem to me like asking which blade in a pair of scissors is most necessary. A serious moral effort is the only thing that will bring you to the point where you throw up the sponge. Faith in Christ is the only thing to save you from despair at that point: and out of that Faith in Him good actions must inevitably come. There are two parodies of the truth which different sets of Christians have, in the past, been accused by other Christians of believing: perhaps they may make the truth clearer. One set were accused of saying, "Good actions are all that matters. The best good action is charity. The best kind of charity is giving money. The best thing to give money to is the Church. So hand us over £10,000 and we'll see you through." The answer to that nonsense, of course, would be that good actions done for that motive, done with the idea that Heaven can be bought, wouldn't *be* good actions but only commercial speculations. The other set were accused of saying, "Faith is all that matters. Consequently, if you have faith, it doesn't matter what you do. Sin away, my lad, and have a good time and Christ will see that it makes no difference in the end." The answer to that is that, if what you call your "faith" in Christ doesn't involve taking the slightest notice of what He says, then it isn't really Faith at all—not faith or trust *in Him,* but only intellectual acceptance of some theory *about* Him.

The Bible really seems to clinch the matter when it puts the two things together into one amazing sentence. The first half is, "Work out your own salvation with fear and trembling"—which looks as if everything depended on us and our good actions: but the second half goes on, "For it is God who worketh in you"—which looks as if God did everything and we nothing. I am afraid that is the sort of thing we come up against in Christianity. I am puzzled, but I am not surprised. You see, we are now trying to understand, and to separate into water-tight compartments, what exactly God does and what man does when God and man are working together. And, of course, we begin by thinking it is like two men working together, so that you could say, "He did this bit and I did that." But this way of thinking breaks down. God isn't like that. He is inside you as well as outside: even if we could understand who did what, I don't think human language could properly express it. In the attempt to express it different Churches say different things. But you will find that even those who insist most strongly on the importance of good actions, tell you you need Faith; and even those who insist most strongly on Faith, tell you to do good actions. At any rate that is as far as I can go.

I think all Christians would agree with me if I said that though Christianity seems at first to be all about morality, all about duties and rules and guilt and virtue, yet it leads you on, out of all that, into something beyond. One has a glimpse of a country where they don't talk of those things, except perhaps as a joke. Every one there is filled full with what we should call goodness as a mirror is filled with light. But they don't call it goodness. They don't call it anything. They are not thinking of it. They are too busy looking at the source from which it comes. But this is near the stage where the road passes over the rim of our world. No one's eyes can see very far beyond that: though lots of people's eyes can see further than mine.